# DOYENNE

Carla Hartzell

ISBN: 9798357018328

CONTENTS

Dedicated to my Doyenne sisters:

Dina

Joanie

Norina

Shamrock

Beauty

And to all my Doyenne kinswomen that I have not yet met.

# ACKNOWLEDGEMENTS

When you undertake a project like this, you realize that so many people have contributed to it.

To the Doyennes in my life:

I am **forever** grateful to my sister, Dina, for her sense of humor, her curiosity, her unwavering love and support, and her determination to make her life better, healthy and fun. She inspires me.

I am eternally grateful to my sister/sister-in-law, Joanie, for her positive outlook on life, her quiet strength, her resourcefulness, her love and support of me also. She is my Cosmic Librarian and always knows what I need before I do.

I am endlessly grateful to my sister/cousin, Norina, who epitomizes the Warrior Woman. Her determination, her strength, wisdom, and her love that she unselfishly shares with me at any given time, uplift me more times than I can count.

To the men in my life:

My husband, Ken, I am lovingly grateful for the balance that you bring to me, and your quiet love that sustains me. Thank you for always being there with your sense of humor and another viewpoint so I can expand the picture and see the horizon.

My brother, Doug, I know you can feel the gratitude in my heart for the lifetime of discussions, laughter and healing that we shared.

To all the authors, healers, and friends that have played a part in who I am today, I cannot express my gratitude and appreciation enough.

I honor you all.

# FORWARD

Life Stage 1 - The Maiden ... Been there, done that. Not what this story is about.

Life Stage 2 - The Mother ... Nope, never been there. No experience to write about.

Life Stage 3 - The Crone (ghastly word) ... I prefer The Doyenne. That's where I am now.

Who we truly are has been defined in many ways. If you are reading this book, then I'm sure you have read all the other books that define us according to the author's experience, wit, wisdom and metaphysical channelings. Do we really need to be defined? Do we really need to have someone else tell us who we really are?

At various points in time, someone told us that we were sinners, that we were witches, and non-believers of the truth, that we were ignorant, that we were subservient, that we were non-existent because we were female, black, young, old, Hispanic, LGBTQ, or whatever the current social prejudices deemed. We were also told that the earth was flat and cigarettes were cool.

Then we were told that we were seeded by star races, that we are glorious spiritual beings having a human existence. That we are gods ourselves, and we were generously provided with the tools, affirmations, and daily rituals to attain god-hood.

I believe that at any given point in our evolution, others have told us all kinds of things. We are still trying to figure out what the truth is. It has taken us a long time to get a handle on this and then get responsible for ourselves - as the imprinting dies hard. And we are **still** being told. And **still** trying to figure it out.

This book is not a how-to manual for women to feel fantastic after fifty. It does not offer hairstyle tips, weight loss tips, grand-parenting tips, fashion tips, home design tips, or recipes.

There are many, many books and blogs out there from brave, incredible women who are much more expert in those fields than I am.

What this is - is a book about life. My thoughts, my revelations, my insights for life after 60. And some fantasy writing thrown in during my more creative spells. It is no one else's but I'm a risk taker (being an Aries), and I'm betting that sometime over the years, you have felt, thought, and anguished over the same things. We all share the same emotions, questions, shock and confusion over life.

I wish I could state (the bait and hook line) *if you're reading this book, there is a reason - that you were meant to - that you will find untold truths and answers to your own life questions - that life will then become magical, fulfilled, you will lose 50 pounds, your family will recognize your worth, and you will have found your way.* I can't tell you any of that at all.

Hell, I can't even find my own way, let alone guide someone to theirs.

I am in my seventh decade. If you've been lucky enough to reach this time period then you have been through all the grief, the joys, and the surprises that we call life. I won't be telling you anything new. Maybe I'll just be commiserating and reminiscing.

There is no rhyme or reason for the writing of this book or to the order or symmetry of the chapters. Like life, I wrote what I was feeling at the moment and took a chance on publishing.

My language will get salty. No apologies, that's who I am. If it's offensive, please read something else. I will refrain from the "F" word but no guarantees on anything else.

So maybe this book is about my own journey, not yours. Maybe you might find some connections, maybe not. Maybe I'm just a 70-something woman reaching out to find a kinship in my search for answers before the light dims, and I have found you.

Maybe you have a story to write too.

## FORWARD (AGAIN)

Yes I know there is only one forward to a book, but I am a maverick in some ways. Plus having so many decades of "experience" behind me, I really don't care so much about the rules anymore.

I want to ask for your forgiveness.

Words have always been very important in my life. I can feel the life and energy from the written or spoken expression. I have been writing since grade school. I had to write an essay once, and my topic was how the bible is a work of fables handed down through the ages

I was in fourth grade … in a Catholic school.

Yeah, well, you can imagine. I got a D on the essay. The nuns called me in "to discuss this", grilling me in a setting as if it was the most top-secret, covert interrogation by the CIA. At nine years old petrified panic doesn't even begin to describe it. If you went to Catholic school, you know exactly what I mean.

I don't need to tell you that they kept their eye on me for the rest of my days through 8th grade at St. Mary's.

Before you get your panties in a wad, I made many erroneous judgements in my youth. I have nothing against the Bible or any other spiritual teaching. They all have their place in our personal growth.

What I am getting at is I have collected quotations for many decades. My sources have been books, teachers, TV, Pinterest, and many, many people. These may have also appeared on Facebook, Instagram, Twitter or any other social media of which I don't participate. They have soothed me in my times of intense sorrow. They have doused the flames of my raging anger. They have had me hysterically laughing; empowered my femininity; and just generally got me through whatever I was needing at the time.

At the end of each chapter, I am including a page of my favorites. They may or may not be pertinent to the chapter but they will definitely entertain. And maybe give you pause for contemplation.

And I am asking for your forgiveness if any of them are your quotes and I have not given you credit. I apologize. Sadly, I do not know the authors of any of these jewels but your legacy lives on through the readers of this book.

And I thank you from the bottom of my heart for the solace you have given me over the years.

Chapter 1

## NUMBERS

How many candles on a birthday cake?

*Too many.*

How many minutes of exercise?

*Too little.*

How much does the scale show today?

*Really??!!*

How many more gray hairs do I have?

*Oh My God!*

When did these wrinkles on my face happen?

*That damn night fairy again!*

What size are my pants?

*(Sobbing)*

How much more money do I need?

*Better get a lottery ticket.*

How many more years do I have on this planet?

*Not enough.*

Numbers ... the magic measure that rules our lives. Who is this God of Numeric Data? Where is he hiding? Who's really keeping score?

And will someone PLEASE tell me WHY?

*Tell the negative committee that meets inside your head, to sit down and shut up!*

*This is who I am.  Nobody said you had to like it.*

*If your Inner Being adores you unequivocally, then why would you possibly be seeking the opinion of any other?*

*I wonder how much of what weighs me down is not mine to carry.*

*So far you've survived 100% of your worst days. You're doing great!*

*I can choose to let it define me, confine me, refine me, outshine me, or I can choose to move on and leave it behind me.*

Chapter 2

# THE DOYENNE

According to wordhippo.com (my favorite go-to word finder), *Doyenne (doi - (y)en) is:*

*The senior or eldest female member of a group, especially one who is most or highly respected.*

*A person who is highly skilled or knowledgeable in their field.*

*A woman or thing regarded as the finest or most outstanding in a particular sphere or group.*

*One who leads, or is respected, due to age or experience.*

Yup. That ticks all the boxes for me and for you. I don't even know you but I speculate you are in the age group that I most highly respect … mine. Your experience and wisdom are unmatched. You have the exposure, comprehension, awareness and worry lines to prove your intimacy of the battlefields in this life.

But I have to say, I would call many younger women Doyennes also. The maturity and bravery that is needed to navigate life in these times are extreme. These young women have it as well.

It is an elegant pronunciation but then French sounds elegant to me anyway. I find it to be a quiet expression that commands a presence. It does not need to be witnessed but has an unspoken power behind it.

So again:

Life Part 1 - The Maiden … Been there, done that. Not what this story is about.

Life Part 2 - The Mother … Nope, never been there. No experience to write about.

Life Part 3 - **The Doyenne** … Yeah, Baby! That's Us!!

*Your value doesn't decrease based on someone's inability to see your worth.*

*Women are like angels. When someone breaks our wings, we simply continue to fly … on a broomstick.*

*Life is not about waiting for the storm to pass but learning to dance in the rain.*

*Keep shining, Beautiful One. The world needs your light.*

*Sometimes you just gotta get your halo dirty.*

*Don't put out your fire because someone else doesn't understand your flame.*

*Don't be afraid to shine. Remember, the sun doesn't care if it blinds you.*

*Be present. Not perfect.*

## Chapter 3

# WHOSE BODY IS THIS ANYWAY?

WARNING: *Not intended for use by the faint of heart. Not intended for use by the shy, shrinking-violet types. May cause uncontrollable laughter, which may result in uncontrollable bladder leaks. May cause unintentional reclaiming of your personal power which may lead to an increase of self-esteem, contentment and "I'm-perfect-just-as-I-am" attitude.*

*In case of distress, sit as long as needed on the couch with a glass of wine and chocolates.*

**Menopause weight gain – the 6th immutable truth about menopause**. I'll get to the other five in a minute.

I was looking in the mirror, butt naked, and saw myself from the rear. There were wads of fat over my hip bones and alien folds of skin hanging on my back. These same folds reproduced, bore their young and attached themselves to my upper arms and inner thighs.

What? Did I have a body-snatcher invasion of some sort? I just stood there. I heard an eerie, other-worldly wail from somewhere in the room ... and then a blood-chilling scream ... WHERE IS **MY** BODY?

I finally regained my self-control and realized that was the war cry of *The Menopausals* – A Race of Beings that strikes panic in men and total disbelief in most women. I'm sure I'm not the only one out there who has been surprised by this "stage" of womanhood. That was my hit-over-the-head realization of menopause.

**Truth #1: Always wear a mini-pad.**

Not only is my nose dribbling, but every time I sneeze, I squirt from the bottom. I don't even need a cold. I could just be walking, minding my own business, and there it goes. Geez! Thank God for small miracles that people don't have x-ray vision or read thoughts yet.

Does anyone remember the movie *Fantastic Voyage*? A group of scientists are shrunk down and enter the body. I think they are still in mine. Especially when I sneeze. They are right there in my bladder, holding a miniaturized syringe, and I can just hear the countdown:

"OK Boys, prepare for turbulence. Equipment Ready. On my count, 3-2-1, Engage!"

SQU-I-I-I-RT!

I can almost hear the uncontrollable laughter.

**TRUTH #2: Someone gifted me with Harry Potter's Cloak of Invisibility.**

It has happened to all of us – young people almost walk into us, attractive people gaze past us, little kids don't even notice we are there. And the advertising geniuses have forgotten about us even though we baby boomers have the biggest market share of spendable income.

But think about the potential of this. Instead of lamenting the fact that no one sees us or pays attention to us, we can become the most prank-playing age group ever. We could get away with any type of prank and no one would suspect that it's from that sweet, matronly woman there, especially the fart pranks. Well, everyone blames us for those whether we really did them or not. In fact if I hear a toot or smell something even slightly off, I run like crazy in the other direction. The only problem is I, myself, usually start putt-putting like a lawn mower when I start moving too fast. Not pretty.

Screwy digestion is a side bar to this menopausal thing too.

**TRUTH #3: Technology will always be a four-letter word for me.**

Tweet, Insta, Like, iPads, iPhones, passwords, tablets, security codes, on-line banking, self-driving cars, smart phones, touch screens, wi-fi, google it, Web 3.0, Web 4.0, GPS, LED, 5G, RSS, ASCII, SEO, HTML, PDF, DARK WEB ... geez, what language is this anyway? It all sounds like abbreviations for government agencies. Hmm-m-m.

I need to go see The Wizard. If only I had a brain.

**TRUTH #4: Here's a newsflash – Hot Flashes are NOT a personal tropical vacation!**

We started getting night sweats in our 40's and 50's. We tried to ignore them, but we all know that didn't work. Realizing we were approaching the doyenne stage of womanhood (maiden and motherhood long gone), we became paranoid. We vowed that "the change" was NOT going to happen to us so we started pulling out every gray hair.

Secretly hoping to be the youthful wenches we once were, we took up every form of excruciating exercise that tortured our bodies, thinking we could stop the laws of gravity and menopause, and become visible again. We started buying more anti-aging creams and we are **still** waiting for them to work.

Anti-aging became a mission of the highest

importance. The military should really be consulting us because nothing beats The Menopausals when it comes to vigilance, ingenuity, stealth, perseverance, and invisibility.

But then again, 'Pausals scare the crap out of most men. Think about our power here, ladies!

**TRUTH #5: Noodles are just not for soup.**

There are days when my toxic emotions are the blackest of black – usually rage, victimization and grief. I really can't stand myself during those times, and I can't stand anybody else either!

But I came up with a trick – my noodle trick. A noodle is that long foam tube that is used for floating and games in the swimming pool.

I cut the noodle in half. When I'm alone (the optimum word here is ALONE), I bring out my noodles. I flail them in the air, pound the furniture (warning: they will make loud sounds when beating anything). I jump around like a wild woman. The adrenaline starts pumping through my system. I feel empowered and invincible by my rage, swinging my "weapon" and thrashing it about. As raw, savage emotion is unleashed, the frenzy builds and builds.

I can see why some men love battle.

I continue like a wild-eyed, crazed banshee until there is no emotion left anymore. Finally, limp with exhaustion, I usually have a good cry. I am spent, quiet and relieved. Does that remind you of anything?

I am proud to be one of this Great Race, The 'Pausals. Why? Because words like *Luminous, Enchanting, Sassy, Radiant, Dazzling, Exquisite, Invincible, Confident, Independent, Don't Give a Damn, Doyenne* describe the woman I have always wanted to be.

Are we there yet? We may need to talk.

*When I get old, I'm not going to sit around knitting. I'm going to be clicking my life alert button to see how many hot firefighters show up!*

*Women grow radical with age. One day an army of gray-haired women may quietly take over the earth.*

*The most dangerous animal in the world … is a smiling woman sitting in silence.*

*With age comes the inner strength and power of not giving a damn of what others think. Today I'm rocking who I fought to become.*

*Too old for snapchat, too young for life alert.*

*In my defense, I was left unsupervised.*

*At any given moment you have the power to say: This is not how the story is going to end!*

Chapter 4

## AND YOU “LIKE” ME WHY?

Social Media is beyond my dinosaur communication skills and understanding.

Facebook is quite the anomaly to me, as well as the derivatives of Twitter, Instagram, and Tik-Tok. And now the Metaverse. And don't forget Neuralink. (OH PLEASE Scotty, just beam me up now!!)

I have to admit, Mark Zuckerberg is probably the most brilliant man of our time, and yet the scariest.

Here is this kid genius, who also studied psychology, and he comes up with the most amazing form of communication that this planet has ever seen. Utilizing his tech genius with his psychological background, Zuckerberg has actually capitalized on THE most primal need that we humans have ... the need to feel wanted, to feel connected, to be in touch ... immediately.

*LIKE* me on Facebook.

He has done this so magnificently that we can have that gratification light up the pleasure center in our brain instantly. It becomes more addicting than any designer drug or silver needle, and we don't even realize it.

Because it fills all our basic psychological needs, Facebook is automatically successful. It feeds our ego. It makes us feel connected, it makes us feel so special and important, doesn't it? The immediate gratification is so subliminal that it scares me.

But we have MADE it so important. It's just firing away and lighting up our dopamine pathways like the Las Vegas strip. So much so that we have justified it as being fun, ego-enhancing, and provocative. It keeps us in touch and connected via an artificial, electronic circuit that is not biologically ours. We need - no *crave* - to check Facebook more and more often ... just like most addictions. And I am not even going to go into the tracking and marketing aspect that is targeted directly to you.

And now we have the Metaverse. A whole new creation touted as a "virtual world in which people work, play, shop and interact with others all from the comfort of their couch in the physical world". Is it me but what's the matter with the one we have??

O-o-o-k-a-a-ay. So I don't have to feel the sun on my skin? I don't need to smell fresh cut grass or the Thanksgiving turkey? I don't need the warmth of a hug or cuddle from my two-legged or four-legged significant other? I don't need to feel the tingle of a touch, or my breath swept away by a blast of cold air? I'll just stay on my couch and watch this fake life on a screen, and tell myself that this is the exciting way of a new world and, hey, I am really cool to be part of it.

Neuralink, Elon Musk's biotech company, is developing a brain chip to interface with computers. What is the purpose of that? What does a computer need with our brains? How is this going to benefit humanity? Oh sure, I can hear the spin now ... think of the medical uses for it, or the military ambitions for such a thing, or how it will enhance our human lives by creating an artificial world along with the Metaverse that will provide you with unimaginable experiences, joy and the numbing detachment of an anesthetic.

Has anyone given any thought that the potential for this microchip to subliminally control the human population is very real? Throughout the ages mankind hasn't exactly shown itself to be responsible with power of **any** kind.

Again, I feel like I'm being coerced with technology. Not just coerced - herded like sheep without the opportunity of choice and no recourse to escape.

I am trying to communicate that we no longer have our privacy. We are being fed the beliefs that this is all such a great thing but in reality, we are losing the face-to-face interaction that makes us a social species, that makes us human. We no longer have to use our brains or bodies. We no longer have responsibility, power or control. And we no longer need to communicate. Artificial intelligence and virtual reality is doing it all for us. The movie "Surrogates" from less than 2 decades ago does a great job of this potential future.

You think that's a hysterical extreme that is not going to happen? Fair enough. I understand your viewpoint.

I am not judging anyone for using this technology. This is the norm in the world today. There is no escaping it. My beliefs and actions are eccentric now. What I'm trying to convey is **the need to be more discriminating, be more present in your life, make your own choices, take more responsibility for yourself.** You have the power to do all of this and more.

So, again I ask you, you like me - why?

*The biggest joke on mankind is that computers have started asking humans to prove that they are not a robot.*

*How to frighten the new generation: Put them in a room with a rotary phone, an analog watch, and a TV without a remote control. Then leave directions on how to use them in cursive.*

*I am SOOOO glad I was young, wild, and crazy before there were cell phones and evidence.*

*People are excited about the new IPhone but no one has caught up with the awesome technology of using your blinker when you drive.*

*Anyone have plans to stare at their phone somewhere exciting this weekend?*

*I have been putting a lot of thought into it and I don't think being an adult is going to work for me.*

CHAPTER 5

# THE LETTER

Universal Manufacturing Corporation

1 Olympian Way

Skyward, NE 10001

Attention: Al Mietey

Reference: Serial # HUMBDY 122551

Dear Sir:

In light of our previous communication, I feel it imperative to write and explain the circumstances leading up to our initial contact.

Upon receiving the above-mentioned product, it was my understanding that with maintenance and care, exceptional service could be attained. This was not the case!

Functioning parameters were at an intolerably low level. The housing seemed to be more fragile than I was led to believe. In my opinion not only did it lack aesthetic appeal, but its operational systems were awkward and lacked fluidity. Continued practice and use did improve capacity, but malfunctions and temporary failures continued to plague me.

At this point you can imagine my frustration at not even having an instruction manual to refer to ... because they are all in the cloud!!

My search for comprehensive information and guidance as to the proper care and use of this product caused me to pursue many unconventional avenues of assistance. This resulted in even greater complications with the logic circuitry. These disruptive short circuits caused unbelievable stress and emotional upheaval, especially since these malfunctions seemed to occur just when I needed the thing to function the best!

I had been working at this for a very long time, and frankly, I was at my wit's end. I was sick and tired of running after THIS clarification and THAT solution. Why can't you manufacturers make a product that does what it's supposed to do?? Why can't you provide the correct reference material and operational instructions when the product is shipped?? Why don't you people ever return my messages??

By now I was pulling out my hair. Every avenue I sought was a dead end or felt like a run-around. After all these trials and errors, I wanted answers directly from the manufacturer ... no interpretations, no salesmen, no manuals touting confusing dogma. I wanted the Top Brass and I wanted YOU bad!

This was the state I was in at our initial contact, and you became the focal point of the merciless tirade I unleashed. I was blaming and accusing so profusely and blindly that I didn't realize that you actually received ALL my messages!

After what seemed like endless requests, agonizingly long research, and down times too numerous to count, I finally calmed down enough to understand how much assistance you have been providing all along.

In my haste to acquire this latest edition of the Human Body, I had forgotten that I could come directly to You for help at any time. I guess it just takes the Humanity Division longer to acquire this awareness.

At this point the housing has proved more durable than first thought, and occasionally, the logic circuitry needs a rerouting. Even though the internal essence is more complex than I was prepared to handle, the craftsmanship, skill, and synergy far surpass anything I have previously known. The beauty and magnificence becomes inescapable.

I have now recognized that the instruction manual, which was automatically embedded in the housing's center, was geared toward choice and free will. So I have had complete control of this system's function without even knowing it.

The guidance system that comes with this model has proved to be completely trustworthy as long as I allow it to do what it does best … guide!

In closing I just want to say thank You for Your exceptional product, Your unconditional support system and also for Your patience in handling what I had originally perceived to be an unredeemable problem.

I look forward to working with You for many lifetimes to come.

Sincerely,

I. M. Konshus

*This chapter is dedicated to my brother, Doug, who passed away May 2022. We wrote this together.*

*Grief is like the ocean: it comes on waves, ebbing and flowing. Sometimes the water is calm, and sometimes it is overwhelming. All we can do is learn to swim.*

*Courage doesn't always roar. Sometimes it's a little whisper that says "we'll try again tomorrow."*

*Maybe you've been assigned this mountain to show others it can be moved.*

*To heal a wound you need to stop touching it.*

*Never trust your fears. They don't know your strength.*

*Sometimes you just need to talk about something – not to get sympathy or help, but just to kill its power by allowing the truth of things to hit the air.*

*Don't be so hard on yourself. The mom in E.T. had an alien living in her house for days and she never noticed.*

Chapter 6

## THE POWER OF ONE

The Great Being's chest heaved in a deep and anguished sigh.

*This was not my intention,* he noted sadly. *My very soul is in the creation of this beautiful planet. Earth is not just an experiment or a dumping ground! I infused my very essence into her and her children. They were to be the basis for all universal divinity and knowledge, but something has gone awry. Free Will was to prevent interference, but that is not what I see happening.*

It's Christmas Eve across the globe. Santa looks jolly enough with his snow-white hair and rotund belly. If it wasn't for his beet-red nose and the faint aroma of Jim Beam, no one would suspect his condition. The little ones certainly don't so he doesn't worry.

The stores are crammed with irate shoppers, harried store clerks and cranky kids. The internet shoppers are frenzied trying to get same day delivery for their shopping. The delivery drivers are not exactly merry, grumbling about those damn last minute people who can never think ahead and then have the nerve to complain that they didn't get their orders delivered in time. Everyone feels entitled, it's everyone else's fault, and they are going to post a scathing review to make sure everyone knows how they've been mistreated.

Traffic jams light up the streets. Screeching tires, obscene gestures, road rage and the occasional gun or two reflect the madness being played out across the cities. Patience, compassion and good cheer are not even in the vocabulary.

For those that are companionless the melancholy has already settled in like a heavy stone upon the chest. Some are celebrating the season in a tent outside by the railroad tracks or in a shelter. Some are celebrating with the anesthetic of choice ... booze, drugs or anything else that will numb their emotional pain. Some have already decided to no longer participate in this dismal yearly ritual and have permanently left.

*This is working perfectly,* sneers the other Great Being. *I get better and better at it each year!* From across the heavens, the once-mighty archangel looks proudly down upon his accomplishments. *Christmas is always my most favorite time. Those pitiful humans are so easily influenced! Why, hell, all I have to do is get the media to start offering holiday sales and play up the schmaltzy Christmas theme earlier and earlier and we're off and running!* The Great Being sits back, relishing his accomplishments.

*Yep! Nothing gets the human spirit cranked up faster than speeding up time and advertising scarceness and supply chain issues. It's pretty amazing that one little thought from me and panic, confusion and insanity start to reign supreme. All this talk of helping the needy, doing random acts of kindness, unselfish giving, all just add fuel to their guilt! Even God has to admit that I get more refined at this every year. The season of love gets less loving … hm-m-m-m … pure brilliance and perfection, if I say so myself.*

Lucifer settles back in quiet and complete satisfaction.

The Almighty hears those thoughts and sadly shakes his head. He gazes gently back to Earth.

*After all these eons, he still doesn't get it. I never wanted him to go. He is still a part of me and always will be. But he does love to tinker with things.*

With that thought, the heavens opened and a slow, heavy snow blankets the continent. Walking hurriedly a very irate man looked up from his cell phone catching a few flakes on his eyelashes. *Oh just great,* he thought. *On top of everything else, it's starting to snow. Just what I need!* He shook his head as if clearing away the numbness, and took a deep breath in. He let out a deep sigh, almost a moan actually, and noticed that this snowfall was glittering like crushed stars.

With that he put his phone in his pocket, and not knowing why, gently grabbed his partner's hand. They look into each other's eyes, smile and continue walking. They didn't realize it but they were both radiating a calm glow that would not be seen by most people. As others passed them or looked at them, they too caught the shimmer of stillness and peacefulness that was silently contagious. The luminosity slowly spread through the town, the state and the country. Indeed, peace was brought to even the most tortured soul.

The Fallen One didn't want to accept it. He ranted and raved that this is not his choice. *I have the power! God cannot do this to me! He is overriding MY free will!*

*Ahhh,* God breathed. *Yes, Lucifer, you do have free will. And you do have the power. But so does Earth and her inhabitants. And none are more powerful than those that have allowed their minds to still and hearts be opened. You see, love and peace are everywhere. That is why this planet is so beautiful. It was created in love, just as you were. But it is slowly being killed by greed, hatred, judgment, denial and non-acceptance. That is your doing. But I will not allow it.*

*It may take some time, and as you can see … it only takes one.*

*I have complete faith in them.*

*We were all humans*

*until race disconnected us,*

*religion separated us,*

*politics divided us,*

*and wealth classified us.*

## Chapter 7

# PISS ON IT!

### The Story of Me, Mom and Al …
### (zheimer's)

(Nine years before mom dies.)

Hey Ma. It's Car. How are you doing?

*Hey Car. I'm doing good. How are you doing?*

Good. What are you up to?

*I'm making lunch and I burned the grilled cheese. Piss on it! I'm just going to throw it away and have peanut butter and jelly instead.*

(Chuckling) Okay. So how are you feeling?

*I feel great! But you know what? I can't find my black walking shoes. We have ghosts in this house. Did you know that?*

(Chuckling again). No, Ma. I didn't.

*Yeah, they are always taking stuff. I can never find things. I know it's them.*

(Outright laughing now) Okay. Have you seen them, mom?

*Seen who?*

The ghosts.

*NO! But I know they are here.*

Are you afraid to stay alone?

*HELL NO! Piss on it! I'm fine!*

So where did you look?

*For what?*

Your black shoes.

*Oh, I wasn't looking for them. They're right by the fireplace - where I always keep them. Why are you asking?*

(I didn't have a clue)

***CARLA MARIE,*** Lola screamed. ***Get over here this instant!*** As I instinctively jumped up, my blood ran cold. I knew when mom called me by my full baptized name that I was in for some big trouble. I dashed to my mother as fast as I could, but I knew it was never fast enough.

As I ran terrified toward the voice coming from the living room, the screaming went on. **JUDAS PRIEST!!** ***Look at these toys!! Did you leave them here? I could fall and break my neck!*** As I glanced at the small scattering of Tinker Toys and blocks, the tears streamed silently down my cheeks, mostly from what I knew would be coming next. ***I can't believe that you are so sloppy!*** The raging continued. ***I did not raise you this way! YOU ARE NO LONGER A DAUGHTER OF MINE! I'm selling you for a nickel! Now pick them up and put them away!***

Those words cut deep into my heart more painful than a slap to my face. Alarmed, heartbroken and feeling like I was so **very** worthless, I silently walked to the dining room and put myself in the corner. Maybe if I punished myself, mom would stop yelling. Maybe she would see that I was doing the right thing and she would love me again.

Maybe she would see that I was still good enough to be her daughter.

… I was four years old …

My mother, Lola, and I had a very complex relationship in this life. It was truly a love/hate relationship that was so profound it scared me. It confused me more.

I grew up in a very middle class, very Catholic, Italian family. We lived in a beautiful suburb of Cleveland. I am the oldest of three children. My parents, my siblings and I lived with my grandparents. I don't think my childhood was any different than the majority. We had our unholy sins of various abuses but we also had unbelievable joy and mirth.

Mom was quite the anomaly. I could never predict her moods. One minute she could be laughing so hard that we all had tears in our eyes. More often than not, she would rain down fury with knife-cutting words and quick-as-lightning slaps to any of us kids. We never knew when the dragon would strike. In fact, many times I would try to hide my younger brother so mom wouldn't strike him.

That is how I learned to read people's energy fields. At a very young age I became finely tuned to my mother, hoping I could do something to please her. Or if nothing else, brace myself for the tirade and protect my brother.

Lola never did anything calmly. When she worked in the yard, she was a woman possessed. When she was cooking or cleaning, she was a Tasmanian devil. When she laughed, she snared us all into side-splitting, tear-streaming guffawing. When she was caring for a wound my brother sustained, she was a nurse in overdrive. When she was defending her family or herself, she was fierce. NOTHING was ever done normally.

The highs to Lola's emotions took us to the heavens. The lows took us to hell and back.

Many decades later I realized that mom could have been diagnosed as manic depressive, but we never thought that this was abnormal. It was just part of growing up in our family. This was how she was.

As the years went on, us kids developed our own unique coping mechanisms in relation to mom. I suffered from her mental/emotional abuse. My brother was the target of the physical beatings and yelling. I don't remember too much of my sister's. She never seemed to be in the midst of mom's anger. I'm thinking that by the time my sister came along, my mother just got used to focusing her rage on my brother and me and didn't have any left over for my sister. I perceived my sister as being on the outside of the abuse, but I know she witnessed it and has sustained scars from this also. Even though she didn't suffer the abuse like my brother and I did, bearing witness is just as deadly.

We each had our own coping tools. My sister developed a wicked sense of humor. She became almost childlike in her experience of life. I always wished I could be like her. I think that was because mom demanded that we live our childhoods as adults. Over the years my sister withdrew from the family and sought her happiness with others. I didn't understand it then, but I completely get it now.

My brother became defiant and angry for a long time. He would butt heads with my mother, never relinquishing his position on anything. It became his battle plan, hold your ground and not be overrun. My mother would become literally insane with rage, unleashing torrents of hurtful words, emotions, and slaps. I really don't know how he took it.

I became the meek, passive one, always trying to please. I became the good girl in the family. I was the oldest and I felt responsible for my two younger siblings. Somehow, I felt like I had to protect them. So I thought if I could preempt my mother's strikes by anticipating her needs and desires, she would be happy. No matter how hard I tried, I was never successful. It became my most wretched imprinting and that pattern did not get healed until many decades later.

One of our escape mechanisms at such an early age was Mother Nature. We were fortunate enough to grow up in a suburb that was not yet developed, so our playgrounds were the woods and fields around us. Since my parents worked, and my grandparents were too old to chase after us, we found oblivion and peace in nature. Mother Nature healed us. She loved us. She taught us. She became our babysitter. To this day my siblings and I each have our own unique love and connection to the earth.

As I became a teenager, my relationship with my mother became even more strained, turbulent and unacceptable. I guess this was typical but I was slowly reaching my saturation point with her control, her rage, and her emotional upheavals. You know, typical adolescent reactions to adults.

However, in my own mind, the domination and unfairness that I was feeling and the emotional roller coaster of my mother's ups and downs became more than I could bear. At 19 I could no longer live in the same house and moved out. She became hysterical with me. I ignored her. When she couldn't get through to me, she had her friends call me and try to lay the guilt trip on me. When my siblings and I were in our mid to late 20's, she disowned us because we spent nights with our future spouses. When she had family gatherings, my fiance could not join us, which of course made me passive aggressive and I refused to attend them also. When I married my current husband, she was angry and foul on my wedding day, so much so that I was crying on that day because of her! She herself is scowling in every picture. How sad, wasn't it? I let her ruin another moment in my life. But that was the last time … almost. But that event helped me to find my voice.

There are many more tales of insane attempts of control, spiteful words, ear-shattering arguments, volcanic emotional eruptions, pain and hurt that went on between my mother and me. They are too numerous to mention and would not mean anything to you unless you experienced first-hand the maniacal actions of this woman.

Then there were the moments of laughter, loving hugs, sentimental memories, shared thoughts and closeness that a mother and daughter should share. So even into my 50's I still lived on the edge of confusion and uncertainty when it came to Lola.

## LOLA'S LEGACY

Mom was really a pioneer in forward thinking for her age. Due to an argument with our parish priest over birth control, and then a later argument of not being able to bury my grandfather in the church because he hadn't attended mass (regardless of the fact that he always donated money and food whenever he could), Mom was ready to fight the pope himself over these doctrines. Instead she renounced Catholicism and became a searcher of spirituality.

As you can imagine, Lola pursued her spirituality,

like everything she did, with a vengeance. She was in the forefront of the "New Age" thinkers. Of course, she questioned and battled all her spiritual teachers with the same defiance and calculating interrogation of a homicide investigator.

Over the years she shared her new-found teachings, insights and knowledge with us kids. We ate it up. It all seemed so right. We had countless discussions of the chakra energy systems, the energy paths to awareness, the things that are seen and unseen, etc. Granted we knew it wasn't a perfect dogma but it made so much more sense than the doctrines brain-washed into our heads. With her intense search for answers to all her questions, mom ignited the spark of our own pursuit for truth, wisdom, understanding and awareness. Until he died my brother and I would have hours of philosophical and spiritual conversations toward that quest. And I am so grateful to her for showing us "the light."

Another one of mom's great legacies was her determined belief to keep things natural and drug free. Her sister died at the age of 29 from liver cancer. This was back in the early 1950's and transplants were not done back then. Chemo and radiation were the only "approved" treatment for terminal cancer. My aunt's doctor was way ahead of his time and told my parents about Koch treatments and to keep her diet extremely clean – organic foods only, juicing, nutritional supplements, and no stress. My aunt never did the treatment as the AMA chased the doctor to Mexico, but my family followed every other protocol religiously.

My aunt passed away without any pain, and when the autopsy was done, the coroner was amazed that the tumor which was the size of a grapefruit had not metastasized and looked as if it was even shrinking. It was at the point that my mother and father recognized the value of juicing, eating clean, whole foods and supplements.

That became a way of life for us. We didn't go to doctors, except chiropractors, and treated ourselves as naturally and homeopathically as possible. As with her spiritual endeavors, this became a mission in life for mom, and we all shared the latest news in natural health care and healing. It was one of the most enjoyable interactions that we all savored. It became our own life mantra. Mom was drug free up until she entered assisted living at the age of 83. We still continue this lifestyle and are grateful that we are medication free and healthy into our 60's and 70's. Thanks to mom's influence.

One of the most endearing qualities of my mother was her ability to laugh at herself and enjoy childlike adventures. In her spiritual quest, she learned that a positive mental attitude is necessary for our bodies to thrive and flourish. As she aged, she became the poster child for all things joyful and fun. This was a complete turnaround from her early years of harsh criticism, manipulation and rage. Lola became a joy to be around. We learned just how much fun we could have with our mother, and our family gatherings became all the more memorable because of her infectious positive attitude. Her shrieking laughter would have us all cackling and whooping.

One of the most hilarious moments was my mother on the back of my brother's Honda 1800 VTX motorcycle. In case you are not familiar with this particular model, it is a beast of a bike -- all testosterone, chrome and paint shimmer. My mother was game to try anything so she insisted that he take her for a ride, and without another word, she hopped up on the back of the bike. My brother, sister and I looked at each other, and shrugged our shoulders. We learned a long time ago that whatever Lola wants, Lola gets.

My brother put his leather jacket on her, which was several sizes too big. He then tied his stars and stripes dew rag bandana around her head, and gave her his sunglasses. Mom became Easy Rider in less than 2 minutes.

So here is this aged, hunched over, beak-nosed woman in her late 70's looking like she could kick some ass and she's hollering *Let's Go!!* My brother jumps on his bike with his cigarette hanging from his mouth and roars away. Lola is sitting on the back of the bike like she owned the road - no fear and in complete control – while her chariot master whisks her away ... the Hells Angel version of Driving Miss Daisy. My sister and I are doubled over in laughter, watching two proud warriors go down the road. That is exactly what they looked like, and that past-life glimpse was not lost on me.

## SO MANY THERAPIES, SO LITTLE TIME

I was going to write a section about my many

decades' search for healing and happiness because of mom's impact on my life, but I decided not to. Suffice it to say, that I always carried a deep hurt in my heart. My own abandonment issues and insecurity unconsciously colored every aspect of my existence.

I unknowingly was drawn to the latest self-help books, various healing modalities, energy practices, and self-affirming rituals. Because of my traumatic early relationship with Lola, I hungered and searched for relief, healing, happiness and answers to the question of why I wasn't good enough.

Whatever soul agreements that mom and I made coming into this lifetime to wreak emotional and mental havoc with each other, paid off. After years of trying to find the one thing that would work, I realized that all my experiences and practices combined have resulted in the peace and self love that I so desperately searched for. If mom wasn't who she was, I never would have found myself and been on this journey. And in my own fashion like mom, I too crave drama and excitement, and I certainly found it in reincarnating as her daughter.

## COULDN'T SEE THE FOREST

As we all aged, our relationships became mellow, golden and loving. We truly began to enjoy each other. My grandfather, grandmother and father had all passed away so it was just us kids and mom. I'm not sure if age brings the wisdom for that or if it was just part of our karma, but in any case, it was really comforting and enjoyable. I almost forgot all the heartache of our earlier years.

In looking back I saw signs that I erroneously dismissed as just part of the aging process: forgetting where she put stuff, losing money, credit cards, bank papers, not remembering what she had for breakfast or lunch, becoming increasingly afraid of little things. Putting lit candles in the cupboards. Accusing me of stealing her money, her hot water bottle, her jar of Noxema, her title to the house. I became the demon she needed to battle in her life. Getting lost while driving. Making over 700 phone calls a month. Having an excuse or explanation for everything. (She was a master at backpedaling, and we didn't even recognize it for a long time.) She started keying in on the negative news reports which fed her paranoia even more. She began to get frustrated and angry again at the least little thing. Hence *Piss on It* became her mantra.

She was constantly saying how this person or that person was ignoring her or giving her the evil eye, and she had a way of saying things so definitively and convincingly that she had us all bull-dozed for so many years as to what the reality of situations were. If mom said so, then it was true. We learned at an early age to never question her. Plus I chalked this up to her earlier personality traits of constant judgment and complaining. I justified that as people age, their negative traits resurface more dramatically. If someone was kind and joyful in their early life, then they would be a blessing in their senior years. If they were nasty, complaining and vicious, this would be their legacy. Mom fell into the latter category. I felt we were going to be in for a rocky ride. And so we were.

No matter what century, it seems to me that the generations always told stories of the crazy, old lady down the street that all the kids feared. Or the old man that just sat in his rocker and muttered to himself. Or the woman with vacant eyes that suddenly appeared in front of you, searching your face for some answer to something she didn't quite know. We finally gave it a name in the twentieth century … dementia. Not only did we assign a name, but we also further delineated it with terms like mild cognitive impairment and Alzheimer's.

For a long time this was labeled an old person's disease. Everyone assumed that as we aged, forgetfulness was an inevitable trait we somehow acquired. *Geez, where did I put my keys? ... What is that woman's name? … I don't remember the whole drive here.* But then as the numbers stricken with Alzheimer's began to grow and more people talked about it, we began to notice it, and we began to wonder about our own family members.

This chapter is of a daughter's journey who so desperately sought the approval and love of a mother that could not give it most of the time. And it is also the story of the daughter's perception of her mother's iron will and journey into Alzheimer's. Some of it will resonate with you, as children of the ALZ. Some of it will resonate with you because you too have struggled with codependency and self-esteem issues. Maybe this won't strike a chord with you at all. That's okay. Writings from other authors may.

No matter how much people think they understand, they do not. Unless they are living 24/7 with someone who has Alzheimer's, they cannot begin to fathom the mountain of emotions that you continuously ascend and descend daily.

They cannot understand that the heart breaks and overflows with so much grief that there is a chasm that will always be raw.

They cannot understand that stress and worry causes all kinds of chemical and emotional reactions in your brain and your body, causing you to do and say things that are not like you.

They cannot understand the intensity of frustration and rage that consumes you and erupts in such violent, black thoughts that they scare the crap out of you because you are afraid that you will act on them.

And then you become guilty and ashamed for thinking about them.

They just cannot understand. And it's OK.

There were times that I didn't understand why my family could be so unresponsive to my hysterical rants about mom so I became very angry. They are not meant to understand what you are going through – it is your experience - but they will support you to the best of their ability. Even if they abandon you, that is to the best of their ability. It may not be what you want or need, but again, their journey is their own.

I have walked this path and know what you are feeling. My one purpose in writing this chapter is to let you know that you are not alone in your guilt, your anger, your confusion, your fear and your shame regarding second guessing yourself in dealing with an Alzheimer's relative. No one else is walking in your shoes and you are perfectly within your right to experience this situation in whatever capacity you need to. There are no judgments here, so please don't judge yourself.

I hold nontraditional opinions as to the cause of Alzheimer's, at least in my mother's case. I am not medically trained, but I am very intuitive. I can read people's energies, and as with most victims of abuse, I am empathic. You unconsciously learn these traits in order to survive.

My mother had many emotional demons. Her life was a constant battle for recognition and love. Since her death, I have done many hours of healing between us and I am at peace with our relationship … and so is mom.

If you have someone that has been touched by Alzheimer's or mental instability, take them to be tested. Don't let the fear of the unknown paralyze you. You will be better able to cope with a definite diagnosis.

If you are in the middle of caring for someone with Alzheimer's my heart goes out to you. There are many resources available even though I know you are so overwhelmed right now that you just cannot think about one more thing. Don't make the mistake I did and not use them. Please reach out … to anyone.

Finally, if you have lost a loved one to ALZ, take a deep breath and know **that whatever you did … whatever you didn't do …**

**IT WAS ENOUGH**

*The loneliest moment in someone's life is when they are watching their whole world fall apart.*

*My dark days made me strong, or maybe I was already strong, and they made me prove it.*

*A strong person is someone who is quiet and sheds tears for a moment, then picks up the sword and fights again.*

*Never complain about what your parents couldn't give you. It was probably all they had.*

*What doesn't kill you, gives you a lot of unhealthy coping mechanisms and a really dark sense of humor.*

*There is more money being spent on boob jobs and Viagra than on Alzheimer's research, which means by 2040, the elderly will have perky boobs, stiff willies, and no idea why.*

Chapter 8

# INNOCENCE LOST

Leprechauns, fairy dust, magical mushrooms ... not the kind of everyday thoughts that a well organized, somewhat compulsive woman usually has going through her mind. But that's just what happened. Driving home from work, stuck in a construction delay on this pleasantly warm September afternoon, a flower dustball gently floated into my motionless car. Without even meaning to, I was caught up in the gentle whimsey of its movements. Maybe it was because traffic was at a standstill. Or maybe it's because I didn't even detect a breeze and was surprised, that at this very still minute of my life, this feathery lightness was blissfully dancing on the invisible air currents within my car.

For a few brief minutes I was transported back to being a child of five. It was the first summer of our move to the suburbs from Cleveland. Our swingset was in a cleared path of our wooded backyard. I remember how neat it was, swinging as high as I could in the protection of the shade trees with sunlight streamers all around me.

Then I saw it. Something on the ground under the trees caught my eye. It sparkled and glittered in the sunlight. I just had to jump off my swing to see what it was! It could be dropped coins, lost diamonds or stolen pirate booty – after all, the mind of a five-year old knows no bounds! As I got closer, I let out a squeal. It was the biggest, most beautiful mushroom I had ever seen in my entire five years! A brilliant red velvet cap covered its snow-white gills and stalk. But what was even more captivating were the diamond-like flecks that dotted the crimson dome. I couldn't stop looking at it!

With thoughts of picking it for my mother, I stooped to get a closer look. I gasped! A little person stepped from behind the enchanted mushroom. He tipped his hat and smiled at me!

Now mind you, even at five years old I had the logical mind of a toddler Spock. I mean, even Peter Pan was just a fairy tale, right? Who in their right mind didn't want to grow up! (OK, I admit … I did think it would be pretty neat to fly though).

It's pretty amazing the rapid-fire thoughts that go through a youngster's mind caught in the throes of reality vs. fantasy. I remember I covered my mouth, half in fright, half not to make sounds to scare this little person away. *OK*, I thought, *this is just my imagination. If I close my eyes real tight, then he'll go away.* Well, I did just that except this little leprechaun didn't go away! It's like he read my mind and started laughing at me – not a little smirky, tee-hee laugh, but a mischievous, belly-shaking, bent over kind of laugh!

That did it!! I made a beeline for the house. While running my young mind was desperately trying to figure out how to tell my mother what I saw. What should I say? That there's a leprechaun living under the mushrooms in our backyard? Yeah, right.

But what if it wasn't true? I shuddered to think what Lola would do to me for lying. As I ran panting up the back steps, through the door and into the kitchen, I knew what must be done.

*The secret of that beautiful mushroom <u>must</u> be kept from the grownups!!*

Even though it took only moments, it seemed like a very long time to calm myself down enough to go back out. I warily walked back to the swingset. I glanced at the mushroom. It was still there, but no little person. I gingerly approached it and began a careful inspection to see where he was hiding. Gone … vanished … kaput!

A sense of sadness came over me. I lost the moment … that one magical moment to be able to communicate with the fantasy world. Even though I considered myself a grownup kid, I secretly yearned to really believe in Peter Pan, fairies and leprechauns. But now that he is gone, from just one moment of not believing, I put myself officially into the world of adult reality.

Traffic started moving again and broke my reverie. A quiet sense of nostalgia came over me and I realized what this was all about. Sometimes as grownups we forget that other worlds exist – worlds of magic, fantasy, childlike wonder and very special secrets. You may believe all the cliches describing our hectic, monotonous lives as true, however, each one of us has a magical memory. Going back to that special memory brings a lightness to our hearts that adds balance to our lives.

Yes, this is a true story. Yes, no matter where I am, I still look for that beautiful mushroom, and yes, if I ever see that little guy again, you can bet I'm NOT going to blink my eyes and run away!

Who knows, if you look hard enough, he may have skipped to YOUR backyard.

*Those that don't believe in magic will never feel it.*

*Once in a while, in the middle of ordinary life,
We are given a fairy tale.*

*It is important to remember that we all have magic inside us.*

*Live for the moments you can't put into words.*

*The question is not what you look at but what you see.*

*Someone told me I was delusional. I almost fell off my unicorn.*

Chapter 9

# AN UNCOMMON SISTERHOOD

The year is 2008. Two years earlier my husband moved to Arizona for a job. I chose to stay in Ohio to care for aging relatives until they moved onto their next journey. One of them was my mother who had Alzheimer's. That in itself is a story that only children of the ALZ will painfully carry in their hearts, but that is not the story I'm telling today.

I moved in with my mother in 2006, knowing the next couple years were going to be difficult for me as a caretaker of not only my challenging mother, but also of two very demanding uncles, who were in the process of making the transition to their next lives. But as the saying goes, when one door closes, another opens.

That open door brought me a young, small doe meandering up from the woods, slowly making her way past the picnic table toward the house. I give her the "sign" as I learned in Monty Roberts' book *The Man Who Listens to Horses*, putting my hands up to the side of my head and flicking them back and forth as if they were deer ears prickling at every sound.

She stops. I hold my breath hoping it's her. She continues toward me and even speeds up her gate. I gasp. *It's her! It's her!*

I have always been an animal lover and voraciously read books on animals and how to communicate with them. I secretly envied those people that have that special connection with nature, those that can communicate with animals, trees, devas and nature spirits. I have always wished to be one of them.

Monty Roberts' personal story in *The Man Who Listens to Horses* impacted me years ago. He actually gave tips on how to communicate with critters. None of the mumbo-jumbo, clear your mind, gain inner peace stuff. Now mind you, I am a firm believer in the non-world reality, the unseen, energy healing, and the whole controversial ball of wax. However, Monty's instructions were down-to-earth, solid steps. I was excited to have something concrete to try.

For over a decade I prayed for a chance to try out

Monty's tips, and whenever I was in the woods and saw deer, I did "the sign". He is right. They get curious and do follow you … to a point.

The Sign consists of putting my hands on either side of my head, thumbs pointing to my skull, the rest of my fingers held close together, straight and slightly cupped. I would rotate or flick one at a time like the deer trying to radar in on something. I would slowly walk toward them. You definitely get their attention. They stand perfectly still, very confused and ready for flight at any moment. But the look they exude is hilarious, or maybe it's the energy they're giving off. It's almost as if they're saying, *Yup, Here we go again, boys. Another one trying to lure us in.*

I am very wary that in a heartbeat they may flee in panic, and just at the moment when I think they will fly out of here, I turn my back to them and put my hands behind me over my butt. I flick my fingers up and down as if I'm flicking my "tail". Then I start walking away. Monty is absolutely correct. Their curiosity gets the best of them and they do start to follow you.

Now if you haven't seen this behavior in a human

before, it does look pretty ridiculous and downright funny. My mother panicked the first time she saw me do this in the yard, but she was at that stage of Alzheimer's where unrealistic fears were settling in.

Mom called me from the back door and asked what I'm doing. I told her I'm talking with the deer. Her face goes ashen. She said come inside. I told her not yet. I then turned and flicked my tail. Her eyes widened and her voice went up an octave as she yelled my name. That's when I saw the fear in her eyes. I knew she thought I was having a nervous breakdown. I was torn. I was really making headway with this herd of deer, but my 80 year old, dementia mother was going to stroke out if I kept this up. I couldn't do this to her. By that time the herd had scattered so I reluctantly gave up my signing and went inside.

Mom quietly asked me again what I was doing, her eyes searching my face for some sign of mental stability – which was quite ironic, given her condition. Again, I told her I was talking with the deer. Well, it took me about a half hour to try to explain to this confused, degenerating mind what I was trying to do. She finally admitted that she thought she was going to have to call an ambulance because she felt I was losing it. That irony was not lost on me.

I had been feeding this beautiful doe for several weeks now and couldn't come up with a name. Mom suggested just calling her Beauty, and I did. The name fits perfectly.

I had been enticing Beauty to come closer to me by throwing the apple pieces out to her, then gradually throwing them shorter distances. I was in awe of her beauty: the eyes that are so huge, the incredibly long eyelashes, the pencil-thin legs that do not seem strong enough to support her body, the color of her fur.

That closed door opened wider for me. The complexities, frustrations, and fears of taking care of my mother and my uncles disappeared whenever I saw her.

Beauty never took her eyes off me while she ate. She came around 2-3 times a day and would wait at the bottom of the patio steps. Mom also started to feed her when I wasn't there. Even through her Alzheimer's, mom never lost her own love of animals.

One time as I was working in the garden with my back to the woods, I felt this presence. I turned around and there was Beauty, watching me, patiently waiting to be fed. I slowly walked back up to the house. She followed behind and waited at the bottom of the patio steps for her apples. I was overjoyed! We crossed a boundary. We created a silent partnership!

Over the course of the next few months I gradually was able to draw Beauty closer to me. For a long while she would only feed a few feet from me. Then in early July, instead of throwing the food to her, I held the apples in my open palm, I became motionless. Beauty wasn't sure what to make of it. She got about three feet from me, stomped her hoof, and shook her head. She wanted those apples but not from my hand. I wouldn't give in. Two very determined, stubborn women ... one human, one animal. Really not much difference between species.

Then very slowly, she came up to me. She sniffed and ate the apple pieces right out of my hand. I was so excited I could barely contain myself, but I knew if I showed the slightest movement she would bolt. I just couldn't believe that I actually accomplished that! Just to make sure it wasn't a fluke thing, I filled my palm three more times at that feeding. She then had enough and wandered off.

Since that encounter, I had been feeding her right out of my hand several times a day. It was one of the most joyful experiences and connections I have ever had in this lifetime. Thank God I had a great zucchini crop that summer because I supplemented the apples with zucchini, blueberries, overripe bananas, strawberries, and an occasional graham cracker. Beauty became our living vessel for scrap fruits and vegetables of any kind. When I would run out of stuff at the house, I would make a quick beeline to the local market and get several-days-old produce just to keep her returning to the back door.

Beauty remained really thin for most of the summer. The flies and insects were merciless to her. Hundreds were constantly feeding on her, probably due to her compromised immune system. One day she arrived and I was horrified to see her condition. She was bleeding in dozens of areas all over her body. Her fur was literally torn from her. Raw, oozing flesh was exposed all over. I couldn't grasp what happened. Then it dawned on me – she was biting her own body because of the insects. I then noticed a large lump on the side of her jaw.

I was mortified. I got on the internet and scoured for deer diseases. I was frantic. What could I do to save this beautiful creature? I prayed to every God and Goddess, every Being, every religious Entity that I could think of to help her heal. I tried to help in my own primitive way. I sent her prayers and energy healing, anything to help this suffering creature.

She didn't come around for a week, and I was devastated. I cried over her like I anguished for my own dogs when I had to put them down. I just couldn't bear the thought that I wouldn't see her again. Where was she? What happened to her? She added so much joy to my day. She was the calm, the comfort and the beauty that sustained me through these trying times with my family. My heart ached and broke. I mourned many times throughout the day, day after day. My grief was no less than that of losing a family member to death. She was my only bright spot in a lonely life of constant caregiving and stress.

After the longest seven days of my life, Beauty finally came around again. I felt like I was given a miracle, a second chance. The tears I shed at that moment were definitely not the grieving kind.

Now that she came back, my care-giver instincts kicked in and I had to try to "save" her. I couldn't lose her again. I was too beat up from the emotional toll of that loss earlier. Her body was still raw and bleeding so I then came up with the idea of giving her colloidal silver to help her heal. I figured if it was OK for humans, it should be OK for her. (I never said I had Spock's logic). I soaked her apple pieces in it and gave it to her for two weeks. I went through about six ounces of silver during that time. I wasn't sure if it would help but it sure couldn't hurt. Her hide healed nicely, and the lump on the side of her jaw bled open and reduced in size. Before that happened I noticed she couldn't eat large pieces of food very easily so my daily ritual changed to cutting them into bite-sized pieces. My care-giving duties now evolved to include wildlife. As I took care of Beauty, she became the child I never had.

I've had a few eye-opening experiences with how quickly the temperament of a deer can turn. Bo-Bo is a boxy young doe that also came into the yard. One time, as I was feeding Beauty, Bo-Bo came up to me also. I extended my other hand to her with food. In a heartbeat, Beauty turned, inches from me, reared up and pummeled Bo-Bo with her front hooves. With a sudden swish of wind and heavy thud of striking hooves, I wasn't sure what was happening. The swiftness and power caused my jaw to drop and my eyes became saucers. Snorting, she chased Bo-Bo back into the woods. After that startling display of aggression, Beauty nonchalantly came back to eating from my hand, as gently as ever. It was as simple as that.

It humbled me to realize those razor-sharp hooves could attack me at any moment also, but for some reason, I never worried. We had that unspoken trust between us.

Very early August I noticed that she was losing her fur. Again I panicked. I thought she was getting sick again. I could *not* lose her at this point. Once more I called on all the Great Beings to help and I sent her energy healing and protection. After two agonizing weeks of uncontrollable worry, I realized what was happening and felt pretty stupid. I didn't realize that deer molt. DUHHHH ! However it seemed to me that molting the first week in August seemed awfully early to be getting a winter coat.

Then it dawned on me! We were going to have a very early winter. In September I started supplementing Beauty's food with sunflower seeds, hoping she makes it through the season. She was still the frailest of the herd.

I started winterizing the house, getting the firewood, stocking up on the basics for mom and me. Sure enough the weather in this part of Ohio got nasty the last week in October.

It became a relentless winter of snow, lake effect storms, cold and ice. I realized nature always gives us signs. We just need to tune in. Thanks to Beauty, we were prepared.

Mom would get a little unglued when Beauty would saunter around the patio. She was afraid she would come through the large picture windows. But it is the funniest thing to see a deer meandering around, looking in like she's window shopping, and checking to see what's taking us so long. This is a daily ritual with Beauty, several times a day, and now Buxton, her male fawn is getting brave enough to venture onto the patio steps too. That's when you heard my mother praying to the deities in Italian.

One day our bond was cemented. On Thanksgiving morning, Beauty came up to be fed. I dashed outside as usual, sat on the steps, and started to feed her. As I was putting my hand in the bag to grab some food, Beauty gave me *her* sign – the ultimate approval from the animal kingdom: *she sniffed my face and flicked my hair with her nose.* This sign of affection is something I had seen her do with her fawn. It surprised me but it also seemed perfectly natural to me. Our interspecies connection was unmistakable. She then proceeded to eat ravenously from my hand. Beauty did this gesture on several more occasions since then. A day of Thanks and Giving – nothing was more appropriate.

As the months rolled on, of course times changed. I continued to feed Beauty as long as I lived with my mother. My two uncles had made their journey into the next life, none too easily. Mom had declined to the point of needing professional daily care. I moved to Arizona. The Sonoran desert valley does not have white-tailed deer.

During that period of my life while I was feeding Beauty, she became my companion, my best friend, my child, my teacher, and my own caregiver. She helped me on so many levels. I became more patient and peaceful with my mother and my two uncles. My perception of Nature became dramatically fine-tuned. I have learned to be dazzled like an innocent child at the simplest things – the way a leaf moves in the wind, the shadows of trees on the snow, the incredible beauty of a doe's eye.

I finally understood Chief's Seattle's words when he said *we are all connected* because I connected in a way I never expected. I became one of those people that communicated with Nature. When I saw Beauty, my heart leapt, my soul smiled and my spirit knew perfect joy and contentment. Not a bad lesson coming from an animal.

To this day I still miss Beauty. Whenever I see a deer, either in the wilds, on TV or just a picture, I secretly whisper: *I have met your sister and I know you. I know your intelligence. I know your strengths. I know your gentleness. But most of all, I know your heart beat … and I am honored.*

I know they all hear me.

*We have more to learn from animals, then animals have to learn from us.*

*Those that teach the most about humanity, aren't always human.*

*Some things just fill your heart without trying.*

*Animals are such agreeable friends. They ask no questions. They pass no criticisms.*

*The difference between humans and animals? Animals would never allow the densest ones to lead the pack.*

Chapter 10

# PIECES/PARTS

Did I mention that I have a twin sister? No? Well, she's not someone I normally talk about. For many decades I wasn't even aware of her. In fact, I just recently met her. Yeah, I know, that was pretty late in life but things always happen for a reason.

Edith.

Don't make the mistake of confusing her with the sweet, ditzy wife of Archie Bunker. Oh sure, she can be honey sweet when she wants too, but most times she is an insidious little witch. Or as I sometimes refer to her as the bitch.

She's not exactly evil but she is difficult. She intrudes in my life when I least expect it and wreaks havoc with me and anyone that she is focused on.

(*A deep, surrendering sigh*) … Yeah … Edith … my Ego.

Damn, but that woman is absolutely brilliant!

She sneaks up on me when I least expect it and takes total control of my mind and won't let go without a fight.

For instance someone will say something in an angry tone or do something that I think they shouldn't and she immediately kicks in with her diatribe. She goes from zero to 160 mph in seconds. She comes up with an uninterrupted dialogue of what I should have said and then that sticks in my brain and I become indignantly righteous. Edith takes over my mind and thoughts so completely that I become as justified as a hellfire and brimstone cleric of the Crusades or the witch hunts. I become obsessive and unreasonable in my thinking. I become so angry that I cannot do a damn thing except pace the floor and storm and pontificate at that person, who is long gone. The kicker is, that whole dialogue she initially started is all fake … a fake drama. But she loves to see me get all wound up because she knows that it will take hours or even days for me to settle down. Edith thrives on that negative emotion, and I cannot even control it, that little bitch! Once she's in my head, it's like one of those earworms that stick and won't go away.

One of the most insidious ways she makes my life miserable is right before I go to sleep. I will be nodding off in the chair and decide I better get my fanny to bed. By the time I stop to pee and walk to the bedroom, I am wide awake. That little witch,

AGAIN, takes control of my mind with all kinds of worries that never bothered me during the day … *I wonder what the weather is going to be tomorrow. What will the dentist find? Will I have the money for this thing or that thing? Is that pain a sign of cancer? Should I be doing more for my health? Should I get a part-time job? Should I stay more in touch with family and friends? Is so-and-so upset over what I said or did? Is the planet going to blow itself up?* It goes on and on and on.

So after about an hour of this, I know I'm not going to sleep and Edith wins again. I get up. I read. I make lists. I surf the net. I try to use the tools I've learned over the years to quiet my mind. Usually about an hour and a half later, I am tired enough to fall asleep.

But she doesn't stop there. She starts up again as soon as I wake up in the middle of the night to pee, except this time it's usually with the emotions of grief and sadness. As you will read in the next chapter, those are the most agonizing and heart-wrenching thoughts I can have. So AGAIN, I'm up because of Edith.

I have read many books by authors that claim the ego, the shadow self, our subconscious mind - whatever you want to call it - must be tamed, quieted and not allowed to take over our lives. It has been called a parasite of epic proportions. It needs to be shut down, gone, and gotten rid of if we want to be happy. Doesn't this sound like what humanity has always done on this planet ... subjugate or obliterate whatever does not fit into the current realm of acceptance? Or whatever we are afraid of?

That philosophy makes absolutely no sense to me. I mean, why should we get rid of something that is an intrinsic part of ourselves? It's like getting a lobotomy for a headache!

So being the good little rule follower that I have been all my life, I believed what these people were saying. And for some reason I also believed that they knew better than me. Over the years I tried every meditation, used every tool, said millions of affirmations, did EFT, Emotional Clearing, sound healing, color healing, visualizations, journaling and became a double Reiki Master. I did thousands of healings on myself and pursued healing sessions from others that I thought were more proficient in the healing arts or more "in tune" with the Divine than I was. I have read dozens of self-help books and have had countless discussions with family and friends over the latest, new-found publication. I pursued energy work like a born-again zealot to try to feel better and get my negative ego emotions under control. I spent many, many hours trying to figure out why none of this was permanently working. I'm doing all the things "they" said to do. I tearfully beseeched God, the entire hierarchy of angels, all my guides and any other Being I could think of to please help me and release me from this brutal cycle. I was sick and tired of that negative programming and I wanted no more of it!!

Many decades ago I read a series of books called *Right Use of Will* by Ceanne DeRohan. It was a very difficult to understand series but I kept plugging away at it thinking that the seeds of knowledge and enlightenment will be planted, and I will understand the truths of this life.

I honestly can say that at this point I do not consciously know what all has taken root, but the one thing that always stuck with me is that the Creator was trying to get the point across about claiming all our pieces/parts in this lifetime.

Over the years I have realized that we are SO many pieces/parts: masculine feminine; human divine; mental emotional intellectual; consciousness subconsciousness ego; mind body spirit; and so much more.

I finally realized a few things. First of all, “they” do not have all the answers. I need to listen to myself and pick and choose what resonates with me, apply them if I choose to and then discard them when they don't serve me. Secondly, Edith will ALWAYS be with me. She is one of my pieces/parts that I ignored, judged to be evil, and feared because of her power over me. Thirdly, by trying to ignore or eliminate the screaming Edith (the ego), she only gets worse. Sure maybe things quiet down for a little while, but she will raise her head and turn up the volume until she gets what she wants ... acknowledgement and love. Just like the rest of us.

Up to this point I have always humanized things by naming them. My conscious self is called Car. My subconscious self is Grace. However, I never named my ego. Thus, Edith was born.

I haven't studied psychology but I have simplified many of the self-help books I read to suit me. Car is that part of me that I'm consciously aware of right now, my everyday existence as I perceive it. Grace is my soul, my heart song, my connection to All That Is. And of course, Edith is Edith. Whenever she starts acting up, I'll give her 2 minutes to get it off her chest, then I thank her and tell her I'm flowing Divine love and healing to her. It's amazing how that calms her down. Sometimes Edith even goes completely silent, which is hilarious. Oh sure, she goes into her tantrums occasionally but definitely not as often or as intense. If the emotion continues to be extreme, I accept that. I look at it and allow it, still sending her Divine love and healing. She is afterall, part human and **all** me.

Finally owning all my pieces/parts has changed me. I am unquestionably calmer, more accepting of myself and others, and stronger in my self-assuredness. I feel more complete in inexpressible ways.

Part of life is sampling what it has to offer like a wonderful buffet. You may gag and grimace over the distasteful things, but you will eventually find what resonates with you. The key is to never give up. Just keep on sampling, spitting out and enjoying the rest.

Even if you have to go to a different buffet.

*The older I get the more I realize I don't want to be around drama and bullcrap. I prefer to be with people who fill my heart with love and make me smile.*

*"It's impossible", said Pride.*

*"It's risky", said Experience.*

*"It's pointless", said Reason.*

*"Give it a try", whispered the Heart.*

*You can't start the next chapter of your life if you keep re-reading the last one.*

*My brain said "crunches" but my stomach auto-corrected it to "cupcakes".*

*I wish I could sleep but my ADD kicks in and …one sheep, two sheep, cow, turtle, Duck, old McDonald had a farm … Hey Macarena!*

Chapter 11

# THE COLLECTOR

The last few years have been abnormally tough for most of us. Covid struck in 2020 with a madness that was never before seen in our lifetime. We are still experiencing the effects.

I personally did not develop Covid but I never took the test for confirmation either. Yes I had runny noses, congestion, sore throat, fatigue off and on, but it wasn't any more severe than the common cold that I usually get.

However, in the year of May 2021 to May 2022, Thor's hammer struck me down in a different way.

May 2021 started off by having to evacuate our condo when mushrooms were growing overnight out of the kitchen baseboards. Black mold painted a section of wall, seventeen feet long, in our kitchen ... behind appliances and cupboards. Two-foot high sections of that wall were destroyed when the common wall we shared with our neighbor was soaking wet because they had a leak. We could not see any of this until the mushrooms took hold.

Unbeknownst to us, the neighbors were hoarders. They had stuffed the leak with old socks and newspapers and continued to live happily in their own stockpilings of garbage, filth and water.

You cannot begin to imagine the shock of this. We had 24 hours to pack up our things and move out. The anger and frustration of all of this took me to a level I had not experienced before.

We lived in another unit for a month while the demo and reconstruction took place. During that time I found that I had breast cancer. I live my life in my own way so I handled this very non-traditionally. To this day I am very confident in my health and healing abilities.

Two months later in July I was told my brother had stage 3 lung cancer. My brother and I are very close so this came as a shock. I was more devastated for him with his cancer than for me and my cancer.

Three months later in October I flew over two thousand miles (I hate flying) to Ohio to put an elderly aunt with dementia into assisted living, clean out her home (another hoarder), and put it up for sale. Thank God for my sister and sister-in-law helping me with this, but it was still a frustrating, fatiguing and anxiety-producing event.

Five months later in March of 2022, my brother was deteriorating rapidly. I flew back to Ohio to be with him. When I got there, I knew he wouldn't see his 70th birthday in December. I spent over two weeks with him and my sister-in-law, doing what I could to ease this frightening situation the best I could and spend time with them both.

I flew back home, but three weeks later I flew back out … he asked me if I would come. I knew this was it. I was there for an additional three weeks. This was the hardest thing I have ever done in my life, and I consider myself to be a strong woman.

After a great amount of suffering, my brother did pass. In watching this, I, my sister and sister-in-law suffered with him every step of the way, only in a different form. Those of you who have anguished over the dying process and experienced the loss of a cherished loved one, human or pet, know there are not enough words to express how the pain grabs your heart with steel bands and squeezes so intensely that you think you are having a heart attack. Or how you drop to your knees with your mouth wide open in a silent scream, clutching your chest, those same iron fingers strangling your throat while the burning teardrops surge down your cheeks, soak your shirt, and you begin to gasp for air.

The hurt, pain and sense of loss is choking the life out of me on many levels. I just want to get off the damn roller coaster!

It has been only a few months since my brother passed. I am still grieving. But something clicked in me. This has been the most trying year of my entire seven-plus decades. If I continue to dwell on all the rage, frustration, grief, and sorrow, my lifespan will be shortened and I will most certainly live my remaining years in depression, sadness, ill health and regret. With many more years behind me than ahead of me, I've decided to have a do-over. I have decided to become a collector … of joys.

Strange thing is, I'm not a collector of anything - not pictures, knick-knacks, coins, memorabilia, nada. Ok, that's not exactly true. I do collect crystals, plants and memories.

When I discovered my breast cancer, I started keeping track of what makes me happy. You know - one of those gratitude journals that everyone talks about. I have done many of them over the years, but this time with the cancer, I found it was the very simple, everyday things that brought a smile to my face.

I also realized that to see all these joys, I had to be very present, pausing a moment to take in the magic around me. It involves the senses. Disconnecting from everything except for this moment, and using your eyes, ears, taste, touch, smell, and heart to notice anything and everything. That's all it takes. Just a few heartbeats. And feel your smile happening.

Here are some of my collections. I hope they nudge you about your own everyday blisses:

Living in abundant sunshine in the Sonoran Desert. A good rainfall and smelling the sage, cedar and mesquite afterward. Waking up at 3:30 a.m., sitting on the patio with my husband, sharing a cup of coffee, seeing a coyote, spying a shooting star. Watching the breathtaking colors of copper, turquoise, butterscotch, and scarlet light up the sunrise. Sungazing at dawn.

Appreciation and gratitude.

Liberating myself from toxic people, places, and things with no regrets. Not feeling guilty for refusing to no longer be a front-line caregiver. Determining I don't have to follow all the "experts" in ANYTHING! Trusting myself to follow my own guidance and intuition. No longer reading or listening to negative news just because it is out there and in our face. **No longer believing the lie that everyone else knows what's best for me, instead of me.**

Smiles and definitely hugs. Cute GIFS. Puppies and babies, of course. A great movie. Optimus Prime. Crispy fried eggs and bacon. The aroma of freshly ground coffee. The scent of garlic heating in a really good olive oil. Barbecue ribs. A really gooey hot fudge sundae. Cookies … all kinds!

Reading romance novels. Learning about energy healing. Searching out knowledge for things unseen. Fairy tales. Bigfoot. Cowboy songs. Tchaikowsky's 1812. Any song genre that makes my feet happy or my heart sing. A diamond studded cosmos in the midnight sky and wondering what else is out there. A thought provoking discussion with family and friends.

Sage and emerald green trees against a happy blue sky. My busy hummingbird feeder. A hot shower with great water pressure using my favorite scented soaps and shampoos. Bird chatter and songs. A good chiropractic adjustment. A really healthy bowel movement.

Cleaning the house and breathing in the energy of the sparkle, shine and triumph after all my hard work. Fairy lights. A good haircut. Being able to walk and exercise at my age without assistance. Curiosity. Clean-sheet night. Junk-food Fridays.

Comprehending what's really important in life. Noticing and Identifying the fake dramas in my mind … and verbally releasing them. A really good soul cleansing cry. Having a serious, no holds barred talk with myself and then LISTENING.

My favorites … starting over thousands of times … A brand-spanking new day!

Understanding that when I'm collecting joys, I do not worry, I am not bored, and the negative emotions seem to disappear. I feel lighter, more untroubled, and I unconsciously beam.

Appreciation and gratitude.

And finally - realizing that **I** am the Warrior. **I** am the Healer. **I** am the Creator. **I** am the Answer in my life!

I am Doyenne.

So … what are you collecting?

*Some people could be given an entire field of roses and only see the thorns in it. Others could be given a single weed and only see the wildflower in it.*

*I've reached the age where my brain goes "I probably shouldn't say that" to "What the hell. Let's see what happens."*

*Not all storms come to disrupt your life. Some come to clear your path.*

*Live for the moments you can't put into words.*

*You cannot control all the events that happen to you, but you can decide not to be reduced by them.*

*Life humbles you as you age. You realize how much time you wasted on nonsense.*

# PROLOGUE

They say writers should write what they know. I wish I had the magical imagination of my favorite authors – to weave storyline, dialogue, scenery, and characters into a wonderful world of romance, science fiction, mystery or whatever. I don't know how to do that.

What I do know is emotion. Like my mother, Lola, I am very passionate. When I love, I love fiercely. When I'm mad, I am tempestuous. When I've been hurt, I am broken. When I grieve, my heart is split in half. When I've been wronged, there is no redemption.

I'm thinking that you have a deep comprehension of these feelings too.

I used to feel badly about my emotional states. I don't any longer. I am who I am and I am still collecting my pieces/parts. I have learned to be more accepting and tolerant of others and life. But the main thing I have learned at this age is to be more compassionate with myself. I am finally unruffled about who I am.

As you know, this is a very short book, but our age group has been labeled to have a diminished attention span. I must be a testament to that as I, myself, get very bored with lengthy compositions.

Anyway, I thank you from the bottom of my heart for reading my stories. I hope I have given you something to think about, entertained you along the way, and inspired you. Just writing this and knowing that you are reading it has made my life better.

If this book has resonated with you, would you be kind enough to leave an honest review to let other readers know what you thought of *Doyenne?* It could help them decide to give *Doyenne* a try. Reviews will also help a book stand out in a crowd, and it would also assist me in gauging my future endeavors. Thank you so much for taking the time to do that.

I would love to hear from you. You can contact me at carla.m.hartzell@gmail.com.

## FINAL THOUGHT

*If you don't see the book you want on the shelf,*

*Write it.*

## About The Author

Carla Hartzell has decided to be a first-time author at seventy something. Savoring the sunshine and blue skies, she lives in the beautiful state of Arizona with her husband. She is a very average, down-to-earth woman who has experienced life intensely either by default or choice. You got to know her pretty well if you got this far in her book.

Carla has been an avid writer all her life and decided to take the plunge and "put it out there." You'll see by the stories she writes that she touches the heart and soul of life experiences.